I0017474

1. Operating System (OS)

Software that manages computer hardware and software resources and provides common services for computer programs.

2. Kernel

The core component of an operating system that manages system resources and facilitates communication between hardware and software.

3. User Interface (UI)

The means by which a user interacts with a computer, including graphical interfaces (GUI) and command-line interfaces (CLI).

4. File System

A method and data structure that the operating system uses to manage files on a disk or partition.

5. Process

An instance of a program in execution, consisting of the program code, current activity, and allocated resources.

6. Thread

The smallest unit of processing that can be scheduled by an operating system, which can run concurrently with other threads.

7. Multitasking

The capability of an OS to execute multiple tasks or processes simultaneously.

8. Concurrency

The ability of the OS to manage multiple tasks or processes at the same time, potentially overlapping in execution.

9. Context Switch

The process of saving the state of a currently running process and loading the state of another process to allow multitasking.

10. Scheduler

A component of the OS that manages the execution of processes, determining which process runs at any given time.

11. Deadlock

A situation in a multitasking environment where two or more processes are unable to proceed because each is waiting for the other to release resources.

12. Semaphore

A synchronization primitive used to control access to a common resource by multiple processes in a concurrent system.

13. Mutex (Mutual Exclusion)

A synchronization mechanism that ensures that only one thread or process can access a resource at a time.

14. Memory Management

The process of controlling and coordinating computer memory, including the allocation and deallocation of memory spaces.

15. Virtual Memory

An abstraction of physical memory that allows the OS to use disk space to extend available memory beyond physical RAM.

16. Paging

A memory management scheme that eliminates the need for contiguous allocation of physical memory and thus eliminates fragmentation.

17. Segmentation

A memory management technique that divides the memory into variable-sized segments, allowing for logical organization.

18. Swap Space

A portion of the hard drive that the OS uses as virtual memory when physical memory (RAM) is full.

19. File Descriptor

An abstract indicator used to access a file or other input/output resource, such as a socket or pipe.

20. System Call

A programmatic way in which a program requests a service from the operating system's kernel.

21. I/O Management

The subsystem of an OS that handles input/output operations, managing data transfers between the computer and peripheral devices.

22. Boot Process

The series of steps taken by a computer when it is powered on, leading to the loading of the operating system.

23. Driver

A program that allows the operating system to communicate with hardware devices.

24. Daemon

A background process that runs independently of user control, often performing system tasks or responding to requests.

25. User Space

The memory area where user processes run, separated from the kernel space for protection and stability.

26. Kernel Space

The memory area where the kernel executes and provides its services to user processes.

27. Kernel Mode

A privileged mode of operation for the kernel, allowing direct access to hardware and critical system resources.

28. User Mode

A restricted mode in which user applications run, preventing them from directly accessing hardware.

29. Bootloader

A small program that loads the operating system into memory during the boot process.

30. Filesystem Hierarchy Standard (FHS)

A standard that defines the directory structure and directory contents in Unix and Linux systems.

31. Partition

A division of a hard drive into separate sections, each functioning as an independent unit.

32. Mounting

The process of making a filesystem accessible at a certain point in the directory tree.

33. Unpacking

The process of extracting files from a compressed archive format.

34. Access Control

The methods and policies used to regulate who can view or use resources in a computing environment.

35. Authentication

The process of verifying the identity of a user or process.

36. Authorization

The process of determining if a user or process has the right to access a resource or perform an action.

37. Encryption

The process of converting data into a coded format to prevent unauthorized access.

38. Decryption

The process of converting encrypted data back into its original format.

39. Command-Line Interface (CLI)

A text-based interface used to interact with the operating system by typing commands.

40. Graphical User Interface (GUI)

A visual interface that allows users to interact with the computer using graphical elements like windows, icons, and buttons.

41. Shell

A user interface for access to an operating system's services, which can be command-line based or graphical.

42. Script

A file containing a series of commands that are executed by a particular interpreter or shell.

43. Batch Processing

A method of executing a series of jobs in a program without manual intervention.

44. Real-Time Operating System (RTOS)

An operating system designed to serve real-time applications that process data as it comes in, typically without buffer delays.

45. Task

A unit of work scheduled by the operating system, often synonymous with a process.

46. Service

A background process that performs functions for other programs or processes.

47. Thread Pool

A collection of pre-initialized threads that are ready to be used to perform tasks.

48. Resource Allocation

The process of assigning available resources, such as CPU time and memory, to various tasks.

49. Context

The environment in which a process or thread operates, including its state, resources, and attributes.

50. Latency

The time delay between a request for data and the delivery of that data.

51. Throughput

The amount of work or data processed in a given time frame.

52. Scalability

The capability of a system to handle increased workload or expand to accommodate growth.

53. Configuration Management

The process of maintaining computer systems, servers, and software in a desired, consistent state.

54. Load Balancing

Distributing workloads across multiple computing resources to optimize resource use and reduce response time.

55. Service Level Agreement (SLA)

A contract that defines the expected level of service between a service provider and a customer.

56. Client-Server Model

A distributed application structure that partitions tasks between service providers (servers) and service requesters (clients).

57. Network Operating System (NOS)

An operating system that provides services and manages network resources, enabling multiple computers to communicate.

58. Virtual Machine (VM)

An emulation of a computer system that runs on a physical host machine, allowing multiple OS instances to operate independently.

59. Hypervisor

A layer of software that enables multiple operating systems to run concurrently on a host machine.

60. Containerization

A lightweight alternative to virtualization that involves packaging applications and their dependencies into containers.

61. Snapshot

A copy of a virtual machine's state at a particular point in time, allowing for backup and restoration.

62. Backup

A copy of data or system files stored separately to prevent data loss in case of a failure.

63. Restore

The process of recovering data from a backup.

64. Patch

A software update that fixes bugs, improves performance, or adds new features.

65. Service Pack

A collection of updates and fixes packaged together for software products.

66. Compatibility

The ability of software or hardware to work with other software or hardware without conflict.

67. Legacy System

An outdated computing system that is still in use, often due to its critical role in an organization.

68. Concurrency Control

Techniques used to ensure the integrity of databases and resources when accessed by multiple processes or users.

69. Virtual Private Network (VPN)

A secure connection over the internet that enables remote users to access a private network.

70. Bootstrapping

The process of starting up a computer and loading the operating system.

71. Debugging

The process of identifying and removing errors from computer software or hardware.

72. Performance Monitoring

The process of measuring and analyzing the performance of a system or application.

73. Logging

The recording of events and activities that occur within an operating system or application for future reference and analysis.

74. Access Control List (ACL)

A list that defines permissions for users or groups to access specific resources.

75. Service Discovery

The process of automatically detecting devices and services on a network.

76. API (Application Programming Interface)

A set of rules and protocols for building and interacting with software applications, enabling different programs to communicate with each other.

77. Middleware

Software that acts as a bridge between different applications or services, facilitating communication and data management.

78. Firmware

A type of software that is embedded into hardware devices to control them and provide low-level control.

79. Bios (Basic Input/Output System)

Firmware that initializes and tests hardware components during the boot process before handing control to the operating system.

80. Task Scheduler

A system utility that manages the execution of scheduled tasks and processes.

81. Resource Monitor

A tool used to track the performance and usage of system resources, such as CPU, memory, disk, and network.

82. Foreground Process

A process that is currently interacting with the user and receiving input from the keyboard or mouse.

83. Background Process

A process that runs without direct interaction from the user, often performing tasks like data processing or system maintenance.

84. Environment Variable

A dynamic value that can affect the behavior of processes on a computer, typically set in the operating system.

85. Shell Script

A file containing a sequence of commands for the shell to execute, often used for automating tasks.

86. Process Control Block (PCB)

A data structure used by the operating system to store all the information about a process, including its state, priority, and resource usage.

87. Zombie Process

A process that has completed execution but still has an entry in the process table, typically because its parent process has not yet read its exit status.

88. Orphan Process

A process that continues to run after its parent process has terminated, typically adopted by the init process.

89. Fork

A system call used to create a new process by duplicating an existing process.

90. Exec

A family of functions that replace the current process image with a new process image, often used after a fork.

91. Signal

A notification sent to a process or thread to indicate that an event has occurred, often used for inter-process communication.

92. Inter-Process Communication (IPC)

Mechanisms that allow processes to communicate and synchronize their actions, including pipes, message queues, and shared memory.

93. Network File System (NFS)

A protocol that allows remote access to files over a network as if they were on the local file system.

94. Secure Socket Layer (SSL)

A protocol for establishing a secure and encrypted link between a server and a client, commonly used for secure web communication.

95. Distributed Operating System

An OS that manages a group of independent computers and makes them appear to users as a single coherent system.

96. Cloud Computing

The delivery of computing services over the internet, allowing users to access and store data and applications on remote servers.

97. Container Orchestration

The automated management of containerized applications, including deployment, scaling, and networking.

98. Dynamic Link Library (DLL)

A collection of small programs that can be loaded and executed by a Windows application, allowing for modular programming.

99. System Restore

A feature that allows users to revert their computer's state to a previous point in time, useful for recovering from system failures.

100. Process Isolation

A mechanism that ensures processes do not interfere with each other's memory space and resources.

101. Graphical Shell

A user interface that provides graphical elements for managing files and running applications.

102. Runlevel

A state of init and the whole system that defines which services and processes are running.

103. Soft Link

A type of file that acts as a pointer to another file or directory in the file system.

104. Hard Link

A directory entry that associates a name with a file on a file system, allowing multiple names to refer to the same file.

105. Virtual File System (VFS)

An abstraction layer on top of concrete file systems that provides a uniform interface for accessing different file systems.

106. Control Panel

A component of the Windows operating system that provides the ability to view and manipulate system settings and controls.

107. Network Protocol

A set of rules and conventions for communication between network devices.

108. Subroutine

A set of instructions designed to perform a frequently used operation, also known as a function or method.

109. Compile

The process of converting source code written in a programming language into machine code that can be executed by the computer.

110. Linking

The process of combining multiple object files into a single executable program.

111. Debugging Symbol

Information included in a program to aid in debugging, providing mappings between the program's source code and its machine code.

112. Kernel Panic

A safety measure taken by an operating system's kernel upon detecting an internal fatal error, leading to a system halt.

113. Mount Point

A directory in the filesystem where a mounted filesystem is accessed.

114. Remote Desktop

A technology that allows a user to connect to and control a computer over a network connection.

115. File Compression

The process of reducing the size of a file to save space or bandwidth.

116. Resource Leak

A situation where a computer program improperly manages memory allocations, leading to decreased performance or system failure.

117. Throttling

The intentional slowing down of a process to control the rate at which it uses resources.

118. Cross-Platform

Software or applications designed to operate on multiple operating systems.

119. Process Prioritization

The method of assigning a priority level to a process, affecting its scheduling and CPU time allocation.

120. System Monitor

A utility that provides real-time information about system performance and resource usage.

121. Graphical Task Manager

A system utility that provides detailed information about running processes, memory usage, and system performance.

122. Throughput

The amount of data processed by a system in a given amount of time, often used to measure performance.

123. User Datagram Protocol (UDP)

A communication protocol that allows for sending messages without establishing a connection, often used in applications where speed is critical.

124. Transmission Control Protocol (TCP)

A communication protocol that ensures reliable data transmission over a network by establishing a connection between the sender and receiver.

125. Network Interface Card (NIC)

A hardware component that allows a computer to connect to a network.

126. Web Server

A server that hosts websites and delivers web content to clients over the internet.

127. Domain Name System (DNS)

A hierarchical system for naming resources on the internet, translating domain names to IP addresses.

128. IP Address

A unique identifier assigned to each device connected to a computer network that uses the Internet Protocol for communication.

129. Static IP Address

An IP address that does not change and is manually assigned to a device.

130. Dynamic IP Address

An IP address that is assigned by a DHCP server and may change over time.

131. Host

Any device connected to a network that can send and receive data.

132. Client

A device or software application that accesses services provided by a server.

133. Server

A computer or program that provides resources, data, services, or programs to clients over a network.

134. HTTP (Hypertext Transfer Protocol)

A protocol used for transmitting hypertext via the internet, forming the foundation of data communication on the web.

135. HTTPS (Hypertext Transfer Protocol Secure)

An extension of HTTP that uses encryption to secure data transmitted over the internet.

136. FTP (File Transfer Protocol)

A standard network protocol used to transfer files from one host to another over a TCP-based network.

137. SFTP (SSH File Transfer Protocol)

A secure version of FTP that uses SSH to encrypt data during transfer.

138. Virtual Private Server (VPS)

A virtual machine that mimics a dedicated server but shares the physical server with other users.

139. Load Testing

The process of putting demand on a system and measuring its response to ensure it can handle expected load levels.

140. System Configuration

The arrangement and setup of hardware and software components within a computer system.

141. Repository

A central location for storing, managing, and maintaining data and software packages.

142. Task Queue

A data structure used to manage tasks that need to be processed in a specific order.

143. Resource Pool

A collection of resources that can be shared and allocated among various processes or applications.

144. Disk Quota

A limit set on the amount of disk space a user or group can use.

145. Dynamic Memory Allocation

The process of allocating memory at runtime using functions such as malloc in C/C++.

146. Static Memory Allocation

The process of allocating memory at compile time, with fixed sizes that do not change during execution.

147. Web Application

A software application that runs on a web server and can be accessed through a web browser over the internet.

148. Client-Side Scripting

Scripts that are executed on the client's browser rather than the server, often used to create interactive web pages.

149. Server-Side Scripting

Scripts that are executed on the server before the content is sent to the client, allowing for dynamic content generation.

150. Cross-Site Scripting (XSS)

A security vulnerability that allows attackers to inject malicious scripts into content viewed by other users.

151. Session Management

The process of managing user sessions in web applications, ensuring data persistence and security during interactions.

152. Content Delivery Network (CDN)

A network of servers distributed across various locations that delivers web content to users based on their geographical location to enhance speed and performance.

153. Caching

The process of storing copies of files or data in a cache to improve retrieval speeds and reduce server load.

154. Load Balancer

A device or software that distributes network or application traffic across multiple servers to ensure no single server becomes overwhelmed.

155. User Interface (UI)

The means by which a user interacts with a computer, software, or application, including screens, buttons, and other controls.

156. User Experience (UX)

The overall experience of a person using a product, especially in terms of how pleasant or easy it is to use.

157. Prototype

An early sample or model of a product used to test concepts and gather user feedback before full-scale production.

158. Version Control

A system that records changes to files or sets of files over time so that specific versions can be recalled later.

159. Git

A distributed version control system used to track changes in source code during software development.

160. Repository Management

The practice of managing and organizing code repositories, including version control, branching, and merging strategies.

161. Continuous Integration (CI)

A practice in software development where code changes are automatically tested and integrated into the main codebase frequently.

162. Continuous Deployment (CD)

An extension of continuous integration that automatically deploys code changes to production after passing all tests.

163. Microservices

An architectural style that structures an application as a collection of loosely coupled services, each responsible for a specific business function.

164. API Gateway

A server that acts as an entry point for API requests, managing traffic and routing requests to appropriate services.

165. Service Mesh

A dedicated infrastructure layer that manages service-to-service communication in a microservices architecture.

166. Front-End Development

The part of web development that involves creating the visual elements of a website or web application that users interact with directly.

167. Back-End Development

The part of web development that involves server-side programming and database management, focusing on the application logic and data storage.

168. Full-Stack Development

Development that encompasses both front-end and back-end programming, allowing a developer to work on all aspects of an application.

169. Framework

A set of tools, libraries, and best practices that provides a foundation for building applications, streamlining development processes.

170. Library

A collection of pre-written code that can be used to optimize tasks and facilitate development.

171. SDK (Software Development Kit)

A collection of software tools and programs used by developers to create applications for specific platforms.

172. IDE (Integrated Development Environment)

A software application that provides comprehensive facilities to computer programmers for software development, including code editor, debugger, and build automation tools.

173. Virtual Machine (VM)

A software emulation of a physical computer that runs an operating system and applications just like a physical machine.

174. Hypervisor

A layer of software that enables multiple virtual machines to run on a single physical machine by managing their resources.

175. API Rate Limiting

A technique used to control the amount of incoming requests to an API in a specified time frame to prevent abuse and ensure availability.

176. Database Management System (DBMS)

Software that allows users to create, manage, and manipulate databases, providing functionality for data storage, retrieval, and management.

177. SQL (Structured Query Language)

A programming language designed for managing and manipulating relational databases.

178. NoSQL

A category of database systems that do not use SQL for data manipulation, often used for large-scale data storage and flexible schema design.

179. Data Warehouse

A centralized repository for storing and analyzing large amounts of structured and unstructured data from multiple sources.

180. Data Mining

The process of discovering patterns and knowledge from large amounts of data using statistical and computational techniques.

181. Big Data

Extremely large datasets that may be analyzed computationally to reveal patterns, trends, and associations.

182. Artificial Intelligence (AI)

The simulation of human intelligence in machines programmed to think and learn.

183. Machine Learning (ML)

A subset of AI that involves the use of algorithms to enable computers to learn from and make predictions based on data.

184. Neural Network

A series of algorithms that attempt to recognize underlying relationships in a set of data through a process that mimics the way the human brain operates.

185. Blockchain

A distributed ledger technology that securely records transactions across multiple computers, ensuring that the recorded transactions cannot be altered retroactively.

186. Cryptocurrency

A digital or virtual currency that uses cryptography for security and operates independently of a central bank.

187. Ethical Hacking

The practice of intentionally probing systems for vulnerabilities to improve security, often done with permission from the organization.

188. Firewall

A network security device that monitors and controls incoming and outgoing network traffic based on predetermined security rules.

189. Intrusion Detection System (IDS)

A device or software application that monitors network or system activities for malicious activities or policy violations.

190. Antivirus Software

A program designed to detect, prevent, and remove malware from computer systems.

191. Malware

Malicious software designed to harm or exploit any programmable device or network, including viruses, worms, and trojan horses.

192. Phishing

A type of cyber attack that uses disguised emails or websites to trick individuals into providing sensitive information.

193. Encryption

The process of converting information or data into a code to prevent unauthorized access.

194. Decryption

The process of converting encrypted data back into its original form, making it readable again.

195. Public Key Infrastructure (PKI)

A framework that manages digital keys and certificates to enable secure communication and authentication over networks.

196. Single Sign-On (SSO)

An authentication process that allows a user to access multiple applications with one set of login credentials.

197. Load Testing

A type of performance testing that evaluates how a system behaves under a heavy load, measuring its responsiveness and stability.

198. Penetration Testing

A simulated cyber attack on a system to assess its security and identify vulnerabilities that could be exploited by malicious actors.

199. Cloud Storage

A model of computer data storage in which the digital data is stored in logical pools, managed by a hosting provider.

200. Virtualization

The process of creating a virtual version of a resource, such as a server, storage device, or network, allowing multiple virtual instances to run on a single physical resource.